World Languages

Colours in French

Daniel Nunn

Raintree

www.raintreepublishers.co.uk
Visit our website to find out more information about Raintree books.

To order:
☎ Phone 0845 6044371
🖷 Fax +44 (0) 1865 312263
✉ Email myorders@raintreepublishers.co.uk

Customers from outside the UK please telephone +44 1865 312262

Raintree is an imprint of Capstone Global Library Limited, a company incorporated in England and Wales having its registered office at 7 Pilgrim Street, London, EC4V 6LB – Registered company number: 6695582

Edited by Daniel Nunn, Rebecca Rissman, and Sian Smith
Designed by Joanna Hinton-Malivoire
Picture research by Elizabeth Alexander
Production by Alison Parsons
Originated by Capstone Global Library Ltd
Printed and bound in China by South China Printing Company Ltd

ISBN 978 1 406 23918 8
16 15 14 13 12
10 9 8 7 6 5 4 3 2 1

British Library Cataloguing in Publication Data
Nunn, Daniel.
Colours in French. -- (World languages. Colours)
1. French language--Vocabulary--Juvenile literature.
2. Colors--Juvenile literature. 3. French language--Textbooks for foreign speakers--English.
I. Title II. Series
448.2'421-dc23

Acknowledgements
We would like to thank Shutterstock for permission to reproduce photographs: pp.4 (© Phiseksit), 5 (© Stephen Aaron Rees), 6 (© Tischenko Irina), 7 (© Tony Magdaraog), 8 (© szefei), 9 (© Picsfive), 10 (© Eric Isselée), 11 (© Yasonya), 12 (© Nadezhda Bolotina), 13 (© Maryna Gviazdovska), 14 (© Erik Lam), 15 (© Eric Isselée), 16 (© Ruth Black), 17 (© blueskies9), 18 (© Alexander Dashewsky), 19 (© Michele Perbellini), 20 (© Eric Isselée), 21 (© Roman Rvachov).

Cover photographs reproduced with permission of Shutterstock: dog (© Erik Lam), strawberry (© Stephen Aaron Rees), fish (© Tischenko Irina). Back cover photograph of a parrot reproduced with permission of Shutterstock (© Eric Isselée).

We would like to thank Séverine Ribierre for her invaluable assistance in the preparation of this book.

Contents

Rouge

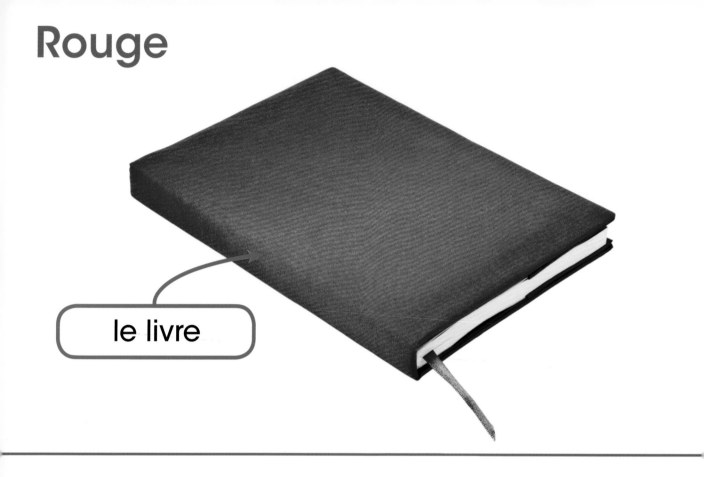

le livre

Le livre est rouge.

The book is red.

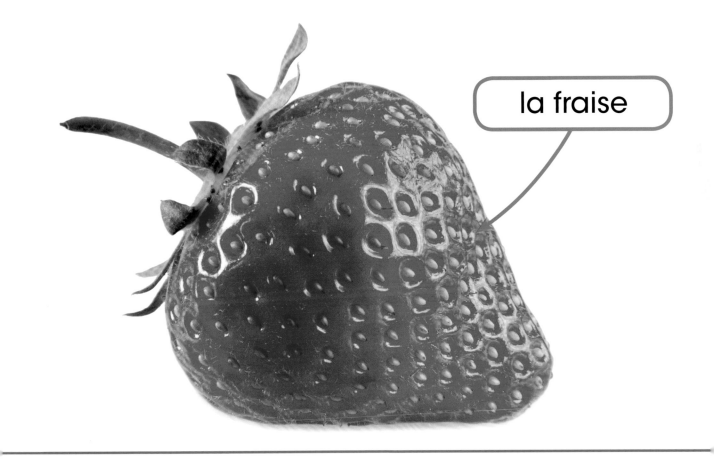

la fraise

La fraise est rouge.

The strawberry is red.

Orange

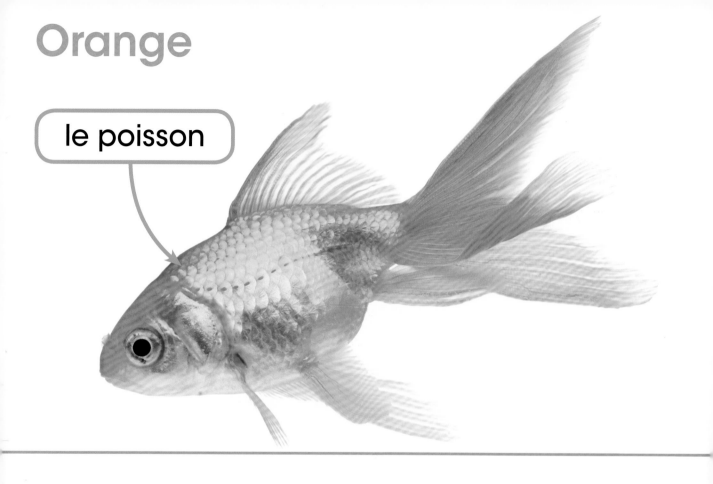

le poisson

Le poisson est orange.

The fish is orange.

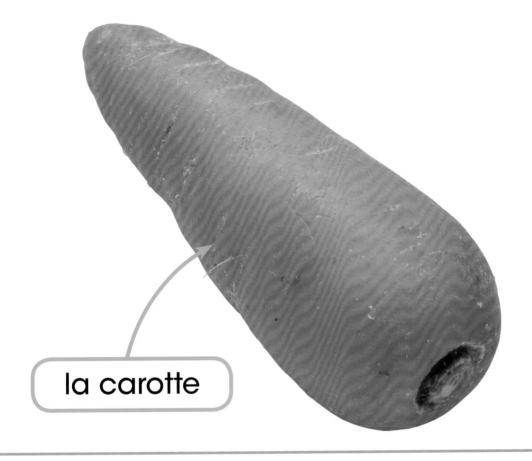

la carotte

La carotte est orange.

The carrot is orange.

Jaune

la fleur

La fleur est jaune.

The flower is yellow.

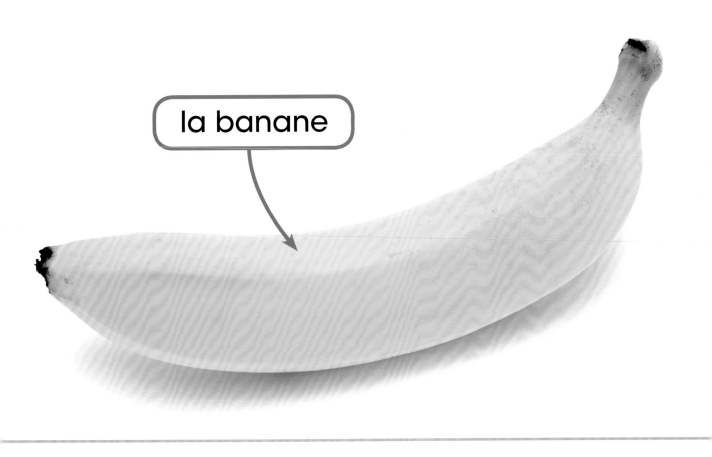

la banane

La banane est jaune.
The banana is yellow.

Vert

l'oiseau

L'oiseau est vert.

The bird is green.

la pomme

La pomme est verte.

The apple is green.

Bleu

le T-shirt

Le T-shirt est bleu.

The T-shirt is blue.

la tasse

La tasse est bleue.

The cup is blue.

Marron

le chien

Le chien est marron.

The dog is brown.

La vache est marron.

The cow is brown.

Rose

le gâteau

Le gâteau est rose.

The cake is pink.

le chapeau

Le chapeau est rose.

The hat is pink.

Blanc

le lait

Le lait est blanc.

The milk is white.

la neige

La neige est blanche.

The snow is white.

Noir

le chat

Le chat est **noir**.

The cat is **black**.

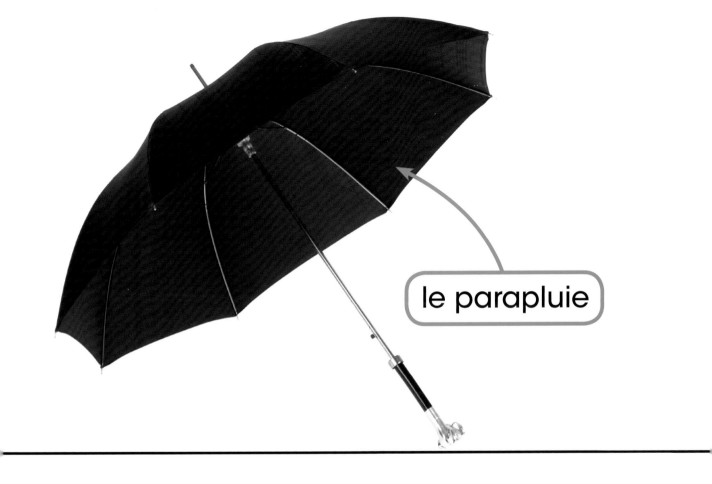

le parapluie

Le parapluie est **noir**.

The umbrella is **black**.

Dictionary

French word	How to say it	English word
banane	ba-nan	banana
blanc/blanche	blon/blonsh	white
bleu/bleue	bluh/bluh	blue
carotte	ka-rot	carrot
chapeau	shap-oh	hat
chat	cha	cat
chien	che-an	dog
est	ay	is
fleur	flur	flower
fraise	frayz	strawberry
gâteau	ga-tow	cake
jaune	jone	yellow
la	la	the
lait	lay	milk
le	luh	the
livre	leevre	book

French word	How to say it	English word
marron	ma-ron	brown
neige	nehj	snow
noir	nwoir	black
oiseau	wa-zo	bird
orange	or-onj	orange
parapluie	pa-ra-plwee	umbrella
poisson	pwo-sohn	fish
pomme	pom	apple
rose	rohz	pink
rouge	rooj	red
T-shirt	tee-shirt	T-shirt
tasse	tas	cup
vache	vash	cow
vert/verte	vair/vairt	green

See words in the "How to say it" columns for a rough guide to pronunciations.

Index

Notes for parents and teachers

In French, nouns are either masculine or feminine. The word for "the" changes accordingly – either le (masculine) or la (feminine). Sometimes adjectives have different spellings too, depending on whether the noun is masculine or feminine. This is why some of the colours have more than one spelling.